VANESSA WILLIAMS

A Real-Life Reader Biography

Sue Boulais

Mitchell Lane Publishers, Inc.
P.O. Box 200 • Childs, Maryland 21916

Mitchell Lane PUBLISHERS

Second Printing

Real-Life Reader Biographies

Selena	Robert Rodriguez	Mariah Carey	Rafael Palmeiro
Tommy Nuñez	Trent Dimas	Cristina Saralegui	Andres Galarraga
Oscar De La Hoya	Gloria Estefan	Jimmy Smits	Mary Joe Fernandez
Cesar Chavez	Chuck Norris	Sinbad	Paula Abdul
Vanessa Williams	Celine Dion	Mia Hamm	Sammy Sosa
Brandy	Michelle Kwan	Rosie O'Donnell	Shania Twain
Garth Brooks	Jeff Gordon	Mark McGwire	Salma Hayek
Sheila E.	Hollywood Hogan	Ricky Martin	Britney Spears
Arnold Schwarzenegger			

Library of Congress Cataloging-in-Publication Data
Boulais, Sue.
   Vanessa Williams / Sue Boulais.
     p. cm.—(A real-life reader biography)
   Includes index.
   Summary: Biography of the first black Miss America and entertainment superstar, Vanessa Williams.
   ISBN 1-883845-75-0
   1. Williams, Vanessa—Juvenile literature. 2. Singers—United States—Biography—Juvenile literature. 3. Actors—United States—Biography—Juvenile literature. [1. Williams, Vanessa. 2. Singers. 3. Actors. 4. Afro-Americans—Biography. 5. Women—Biography.]
I. Title. II. Series.
ML3930.W56B68 1998
782.42164'092—dc21
[B]
        98-41680
        CIP
        MN AC

ABOUT THE AUTHOR: Sue Boulais is a freelance writer/editor based in Orlando, Florida. She has published numerous books, including **Famous Astronauts** (Media Materials) and **Hispanic American Achievers** (Frog Publications). Previously, she served as an editor for *Weekly Reader* and Harcourt Brace.
PHOTO CREDITS: cover: Fitzroy Barrett/Globe Photos, taken in 1996 at the MTV Movie Awards in Los Angeles, CA; pp. 4, 8 Harry Langdon/Shooting Star; pp. 11, 17 UPI/Corbis-Bettmann; p. 24 Shooting Star; p. 31 AP Photo/Eric Draper.
ACKNOWLEDGMENTS: The following story has been thoroughly researched, and to the best of our knowledge, represents a true story. Though we try to authorize every biography that we publish, for various reasons, this is not always possible. This story is neither authorized nor endorsed by Vanessa Williams.

Table of Contents

Chapter 1
"See You on Broadway"

It was evident that Vanessa Williams had several natural talents as a young girl. She could sing, she could dance, and she could act. Her parents encouraged her to develop all three talents. It is no wonder she became the first black Miss America! But the scandal and uproar that followed her from the time she received her crown would have derailed a woman with less courage. Not Vanessa. She fought her way back to become a superstar.

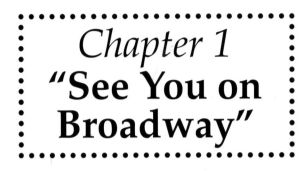

Vanessa Williams could sing, she could dance, and she could act.

Vanessa Williams was born on March 18, 1963, in the Bronx, New York City. She was a beautiful baby, with straight, light golden brown hair and large, clear green eyes. Her skin was a creamy coffee color. She grew into a doll-like toddler whose soft ringlets and smile made people stop and stare at her.

Vanessa's father Milton and her mother Helen were both music teachers. When Vanessa was one, the family moved to Millwood, about 40 miles outside of New York City. Her parents had gotten jobs as music teachers there.

Her parents passed their love of music on to Vanessa. She loved to sing and dance. She loved to play "dress up" and put on shows for her parents. She decided that she would be the first black Rockette. (The Rockettes are world-famous precision dancers at Radio City Music Hall in New York City.)

Milton and Helen never let Vanessa fuss about her appearance. "It was not a point in our family to focus on physical beauty," explained Helen. Instead, they focused on Vanessa's talents.

Milton taught Vanessa to play the French horn and the piano. She took dance lessons. Through grade school and high school, she belonged to singing groups, theater groups, and dance groups.

All through school, Vanessa belonged to singing groups, theater groups, and dance groups.

More than anything else in school, Vanessa loved being in plays and other school functions. Her parents loved her performances, too. Her dad was always the first to start clapping for her and the last to stop. Her mother would congratulate her quietly, "Nice job, 'Ness."

Vanessa's dream had always been to be on Broadway. Her glamorous looks and multiple talents made her dream a reality.

"See you on Broadway" read the caption next to her picture in her high school graduation yearbook. The caption spelled out her dream. Even then, Vanessa knew she wanted to be a singer, dancer, and actress in Broadway plays and Hollywood films.

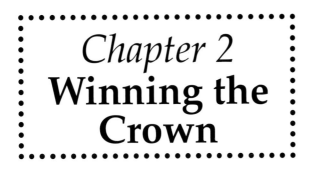

Chapter 2
Winning the Crown

After graduation, Vanessa went to Syracuse University to study musical theater. She also got a job working for a photographer.

Vanessa quickly became well-known and well-liked by her friends and teachers. Many thought she was talented and beautiful enough to be on Broadway.

One day, a friend approached her. He said, "Some people think you should be recruited for the Miss America Pageant."

Friends told Vanessa she should enter the Miss America pageant.

By September 1983, Vanessa was ready for the Miss America pageant in Atlantic City, New Jersey.

Vanessa thought he was joking. She laughed. "Get out of here."

A few months later, though, the director of the Miss Greater Syracuse pageant came to see her. She said seriously to Vanessa, "You've got the talent to be the next Miss America."

Vanessa didn't like the idea of being a beauty pageant contestant. But she knew that the winner of the pageant received $25,000 in scholarship funds. She realized that, if she won, the money would pay for her college classes. She decided to "go for it."

Vanessa won the Miss Greater Syracuse pageant. Then she became Miss New York State. By mid-September, 1983, she was ready for the Miss America pageant in Atlantic City, New Jersey.

Vanessa won the swimsuit contest by moving with confidence and assurance. She won the public speaking contest by speaking clearly and firmly, giving honest

Vanessa is crowned Miss America 1984 by Debra Maffett, (1983). She was the first black to be crowned.

Her winning song seemed appropriate for happy days seemed to loom ahead for Vanessa.

opinions to the question the judges asked. And she belted out "Happy Days Are Here Again" with a huge smile and shining green eyes.

Vanessa won! As she was crowned Miss America, she could see her parents in the audience, where they had always been for all her performances. Milton and Helen were jumping up and down and crying.

Her winning song seemed appropriate for happy days appeared to loom ahead for Vanessa Williams.

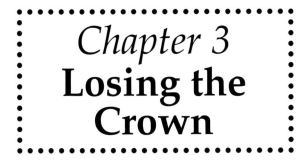

Chapter 3
Losing the Crown

Vanessa was crowned Miss America on the evening of September 17, 1983. Before that night, only her family and friends knew her. By the next morning, all of America knew her. Her picture was on TV and on the front pages of newspapers.

Vanessa received phone calls and flowers from family, friends, and relatives. She also got congratulations from famous political leaders and well-known entertainers.

After Vanessa was crowned Miss America, she became famous.

However, Vanessa quickly became the center of a national argument. Many people applauded her win: she was the first black Miss America. But others said that her win was *not* a breakthrough for blacks. They said Vanessa didn't *look* black: her light complexion, green eyes and straight golden-brown hair made her look more Caucasian—white.

Vanessa thought these remarks "pretty unfortunate." She said, ". . . it's too bad people couldn't feel proud."

Her mom and dad, though, were tremendously proud. They framed a photo of themselves with Vanessa. They called it "America's Royal Family" and hung it in their home.

During her reign as Miss America, Vanessa worked hard. She

She quickly became the center of a national argument, however.

traveled all over the country, appearing at festivals, fairs, and business conventions. She spoke to hundreds of clubs and organizations. She shook hands with thousands of fans and autographed many photographs of herself. She talked with rooms full of school children.

And she smiled—and smiled—and smiled. As Miss America, she had signed a promise that, for the next four years, she would never appear in public wearing a frown! Nearly everyone agreed she was a great Miss America.

Then, in July, 1984, pictures of Vanessa appeared in a national magazine, *Penthouse*. In some, Vanessa was posed nude. In others, she was posed with another woman.

Then, in July, 1984, nude pictures of her appeared in *Penthouse* magazine.

The officials of the Miss America pageant demanded that Vanessa give up her title as Miss America. They agreed, however, that Vanessa could keep the scholarship money, because she had been such a good Miss America.

Vanessa went home to her parents. They told her they loved her and would support her. Milton and Helen then called in lawyers and a public-relations specialist named Ramon Hervey. Hervey arranged a press conference. He also helped Vanessa write the speech she would give.

On Monday, July 21, 1984, with family and friends near, Vanessa Williams stepped to the microphone. With dignity, and without tears, she announced that she was resigning as Miss America.

She explained that the pictures had been taken when she was only 19, by Tom Chiapel, the photographer for whom she had worked. "Based on his persistence and encouragement, and his assurance that the photographs would just be for me to see, I was ultimately persuaded to [pose]."

On July 23, 1984, Vanessa Williams publicly resigned from her position as Miss America.

Vanessa stated that she had never, in any way, consented to the publication or use of the photographs. Again the media said she was a "first"—the first Miss America in the history of the 63-year old pageant to abdicate (give up) her throne. Again Americans argued about Vanessa.

Some said that Vanessa ought to lose her crown and title. They said her behavior [posing for the photos] showed just how loose and "free and easy" modern morals were.

Many others, though, spoke on her behalf. They agreed with Susan L. Taylor, editor-in-chief of *Essence*. Taylor wrote an editorial titled "For Vanessa." In it, she said:

Often in our effort to move our lives forward we stumble. . . . You made a mistake and you paid for it.

Dearly. . . . You're a survivor. . . Even though you've relinquished the title, for us you'll always wear the crown.

And whether or not people thought Vanessa should lose her Miss America title, many criticized the magazine publisher, Bob Guccione, for printing the photos.

Vanessa knew that future days might not now be so happy. She knew she would have to work twice as hard to make people forget her past and see only her talent and determination.

Vanessa knew that future days might not be so happy.

Chapter 4
Starting Over Again

Vanessa stayed out of the spotlight for a few months after her press conference.

Vanessa stayed out of the spotlight for a few months after her press conference. She went to the Bahamas to rest. Her mother went with her. So did Ramon Hervey, the Los Angeles publicist who had planned her press meeting. Vanessa liked Ramon, even though he was much older than she. He had helped her a lot. They spent hours talking about themselves, their past lives, and her situation.

After vacation, Vanessa went to San Francisco to act in an episode of the TV series *Partners in Crime.* When the filming was over, Vanessa, too, returned to Millwood. She felt much better because of the encouragement from the show's cast and crew. She hoped that the worst was over.

But, at home, she got only bad news from her agents. All the offers she had gotten during her year as Miss America—from modeling firms, film and stage producers, clothing and toy manufacturers— had been canceled. For a few months, Vanessa lost her hope and optimism, too. She became frightened. She knew she had to start all over again. What if she didn't make it?

In October, 1985, Vanessa moved to New York City. She wanted to live on her own and look for work. She lived in New York for

She got only bad news from her agents. All her modeling contracts, endorse- ments, and offers to appear on TV had been canceled.

almost a year. She was able to only get a few good modeling jobs. She sang back-up vocals on other stars' records. But she didn't get any good film or TV offers. Her confusion, disappointment, and unhappiness grew. So did her loneliness.

Ramon Hervey was her one bright spot. They kept in close touch. In late October, 1985, Ramon proposed to Vanessa, and she accepted. In another year they were married. They made their vows on January 2, 1987, in St. Francis Xavier Roman Catholic Church in New York.

Once again, Vanessa was back in the public eye. This time, she wore a wedding veil, not a rhinestone crown. She walked down the aisle, not alone, but with her new husband.

Chapter 5
"Music, Movies & Motherhood"

Marriage to Ramon helped Vanessa feel personally secure. She admired his mature, thoughtful personality. He also helped her professionally. He was able to persuade Ed Eckstine, general manager of Wing-PolyGram Records, to give Vanessa a recording contract. She was to begin recording in the fall. However, Vanessa found out she was pregnant. So, for a few months, the recording was put on hold.

Soon, Vanessa had a recording contract.

Vanessa was thrilled and excited. Her daughter Melanie Lynne, 8 lbs. 1/2 oz., was born on June 30 at Cedars Sinai Medical Center in Los Angeles.

Below: Vanessa with her daughter

The next nine months of Vanessa's life were filled with hard work: being a wife and mother, recording songs until they were perfect, filming the video to go with the album. As she worked, her badly-shaken self-confidence began to heal.

Vanessa's album, *The Right Stuff*, debuted in June, 1988. Within six months, the album had sold more than 300,000 copies. Three singles went to the Top 10 on the black music charts. "Dreamin'," the fourth release, crossed chart lines and was played on pop stations.

Again, Vanessa's name appeared in bold, black headlines in newspapers and magazine reviews. Now, she was praised for her determination, her comeback, her talent. She began to enjoy success after success. She became a frequent guest on popular TV shows. In January, 1989, she won the NAACP's Best New Female Artist award. She was nominated for two Grammys, as Best New Artist and Best Female Rhythm and Blues Singer. She got roles in films and some made-for-TV movies.

Vanessa was becoming happier. But her career wasn't the only reason. She and Ramon had become new parents again in June, welcoming a second daughter,

In 1989, Vanessa was nominated for two Grammys.

Jillian Kristin. As Vanessa said in a magazine interview: "I finally have a career and a family. . . [I feel like] I've *done* something."

"But," she added, "I don't feel that this is as far as I'm going to get, because this is just the beginning."

She released her second album, *Comfort Zone*, in August, 1991. Within a year, the album went platinum [one million copies sold]. The song "Save the Best for Last" was one of the biggest singles of 1992: it topped the adult contemporary, pop, and R&B charts all at the same time—the first such triple sweep since 1984!

Vanessa continued to work on her reputation as an actress, too. She did more TV acting.

Then, in 1994, Vanessa got an invitation to the place where she *really* wanted to be: Broadway.

With her career and family, Vanessa felt like she was accomp—lishing something.

Chapter 6
A Dream Come True

When Vanessa received the call from Broadway producer Garth Drabinsky, it was a dream come true. Being on Broadway had been Vanessa's goal since high school.

Drabinsky's offer couldn't have come at a better time. At the moment, Vanessa had no other career projects. Her third child, son Devin, had been born some months before. The family was well settled after a move from Los Angeles back to her home town of Millwood.

In 1994, Vanessa's dream of being on Broadway finally came true.

Better than the timing, however, was the fact that Drabinsky had called her. His play, *Kiss of the Spider Woman*, was a hit, one of the few on Broadway that year. But leading lady Chita Rivera was leaving. Drabinsky thought Vanessa had the talent to take Rivera's place.

Vanessa read the script and loved the role. "It's a powerful role. . . a fantastic role for me," Vanessa told interviewers. "I get a chance to do a little drama, a little comedy, a lot of dancing and a lot of singing."

Vanessa continued her success into the next year. She released her third album, *The Sweetest Days*, in which she sang many kinds of music: jazz, rhythm and blues, Brazilian pop. Like *Comfort Zone*, *The Sweetest Days* went platinum within months.

By 1996, Vanessa Williams had become, as *Jet* magazine claimed, "a versatile entertainer [who] enjoys a distinguished career in music, Broadway, television, and film." And that year, Vanessa landed another great role. She got the female lead in the big-budget [$100 million] film *Eraser*, opposite movie mega-star Arnold Schwarzenegger. She also sang the title song "Colors of the Wind" for Disney's big movie release that year, *Pocahontas*.

Vanessa's performances in *Kiss of the Spider Woman* and *Eraser* proved that she could carry big-budget movies and plays. Like other famous entertainers, she could be hired for roles, and producers knew that audiences would come to see her perform. Vanessa had made it.

She made big budget movies and sang hit songs like Disney's "Colors of the Wind."

Chapter 7
Today...and Tomorrow

Thirteen years after the Miss America scandal, Vanessa felt she was back in charge.

By 1997, Vanessa felt that her career was firmly on track and that she was "in charge." Her personal life, however, was another matter.

She and Ramon had grown apart. Their divorce was final in 1997.

Today, she lives with her children—Melanie, Jillian, Devin—in a big house on a hilltop in Westchester County, New York. She has called the three energetic youngsters the "bedrock" of her life.

And for herself? She, too, is happy. She's gone from a 21-year-old self-described "scandalized beauty queen" to an established singer and actress. In 1998, she starred in the movie *Dance With Me*, where she was able to showcase her multiple talents. She

has set new goals for herself. She wants more. She wants to create a Broadway role. She wants to do more TV movies, and make more hit albums. But, most importantly to her, she wants more time with her children. She declares, "I want to always be a good mother to my kids."

Vanessa performed the song "Colors of the Wind" at the 68th Annual Academy Awards in Los Angeles, on Monday, March 25, 1996. Her song was nominated for Best song from the film Pocahontas.

Chronology

- Born March 18, 1963, in the Bronx, New York; mother: Helen; father: Milton Williams
- Grew up in Millwood, New York
- 1981, entered Syracuse University and majored in musical theater
- 1983, became first black Miss America
- 1984, photos of her published in *Penthouse* magazine; resigned as Miss America
- 1986, first recording, "Hey Good Lookin'"
- January 2, 1987, married Ramon Hervey
- 1988, NAACP Image award; Grammy nomination; first child, Melanie is born
- 1992, released song, *Save the Best for Last*
- 1994, stars on Broadway in *Kiss of the Spider Woman*
- 1996, divorced Ramon Hervey; song "Colors of the Wing" received Oscar, Golden Globe, and Grammy nomination
- 1998, NAACP Image award for performance in "Soul Food;" starred in movie *Dance With Me*

Index

jB
WILLIAMS   Boulais, Sue

Vanessa Williams

$15.95

DATE			